Copyright

—◇◆◇—

Copyright © 2017 Love Kissed Books, LLC.

1st Edition

All rights reserved. No part of this book shall be reproduced in any manner whatsoever including Internet usage without written permission of Love Kissed Books, LLC.

Introduction

Writing is an art, but marketing pays the bills.

Can I get completely honest here?

Here's the deal with this career we've chosen. Ready?

When I first started writing, I was so happy to have selected a career where I was constantly able to be creative. It felt awesome. And I could make a living doing it? Whew. I was living the dream.

Back then...2013...publishing was EASY! I could publish, do a blog tour, and have a TON of sales. We thought it would go on forever. (Or hoped.) It didn't. The bubble burst and for some of us, our dreams with it.

Many of my friends had to go back into the workforce. I didn't have that luxury. Being the mom of a miracle baby meant I had to stay home and make it work. So, I changed my strategy. I looked around the industry, the trends, what was happening.

I watched one author come out of nowhere, and become huge. Some of us sat around and griped about her methods. Look...she's buying likes! (Lots of giveaways.) Look...she's comparing her books to Fifty Shades! (As in...if you liked Fifty Shades, you'll love this series.)

Later, I read an article to learn she'd spent $70k and ended up making MILLIONS. She has book deals, runs her own publishing company and has the success most of us only dream of.

This author figured out something right from the start. It's not enough to write a good book. You have to become a master marketer. Readers have so many options now. You have to get visible.

Most of all, you have to have a plan. Try new things. Try everything. Do it a bit at a time as you can afford. Figure out what works, what doesn't. Record everything. Eventually from all of the testing and theory, a plan will emerge. What works for me might not work for everyone, but I tell you anyway.

Here are things you can't lose by doing:

1. Grow your list. Join every list building promotion you can.

2. Grow a street team/review team. We all need our tribe. Build it.

3. Write a great book. Stick a beautiful cover on it. Make sure it's edited.

4. Publish with a plan. If you don't have a plan, hire someone who does. This next book, I'm working with A PR Company. I haven't hired anyone to help me for a while. I've been doing all my own tours and promotions. (It's a perk.) This time, I've decided to branch out.

5. Market & promote like your livelihood depends on it...because it does. Don't let your backlist die. Unless you've had a billion reads, there are people out there who still need to find you. Help them out.

Remember: The definition of insanity is to do the same thing over and over again and expect different results.

Change it up. Try new things. Be brave. If you leap, the net will appear. If you work really hard, you won't need to worry about a net.

Preparing for 2018

As you get ready to consider what you want to accomplish in the coming year, here's what you need to remember:

1. *There's room for everyone in the sunshine.*

You don't have to shine brightest. Personally, I think we shine brighter when we cheer each other on. By now you should know readers don't love only one author. They have room on their shelves and in their Kindles for all of us.

2. *Success looks different to everyone.*

We're all on our own path. There's no one way to be successful. For some, it's getting their letters. To others, it's based on having a certain number of followers on social media. Still others feel there's a magical number of book sales or monthly income goals.

You decide what means success for you and then...only measure yourself against it.

3. *Keep dancing.*

Failure doesn't mean taking a step back after having taken a step forward. Nope. Successful people know this is a cha cha. Life is just one big dance. Have fun with it. Enjoy it. Life is happening now. Don't miss it because you think it starts when you hit a list, or can work from home full-time, or you make your first million.

Be patient. Be present. Persevere.

Go set those goals and get ready to work towards them.

You've got this!

January

Sunday	Monday	Tuesday	Wednesday	Thursday	Friday	Saturday
	1	2	3	4	5	6
7	8	9	10	11	12	13
14	15	16	17	18	19	20
21	22	23	24	25	26	27
28	29	30	31			

Week of

Goals

Weekly Checklist:
- ☐ Sign up for promos
- ☐ Change prices
- ☐ Order covers
- ☐ Schedule editor
- ☐ Complete edits
- ☐ Upload for sale
- ☐ Send ARCS
- ☐ Set up swaps
- ☐ _____

Monday, 1/1
What to do:

Where to be:

Word count:

Sales:

Page Reads:

FREE:

Tuesday, 1/2
What to do:

Where to be:

Word count:

Sales:

Page Reads:

FREE:

Wednesday, 1/3
What to do:

Where to be:

Word count:

Sales:

Page Reads:

FREE:

January

| Thursday, 1/4 | Friday, 1/5 | Saturday, 1/6 | Sunday, 1/7 |

What to do:

Where to be:

Word count:

Sales:
Page Reads:
FREE:

Week of

Goals

Weekly Checklist:

- ☐ Sign up for promos
- ☐ Change prices
- ☐ Order covers
- ☐ Schedule editor
- ☐ Complete edits
- ☐ Upload for sale
- ☐ Send ARCS
- ☐ Set up swaps
- ☐

Monday, 1/8

What to do:

Where to be:

Word count:

Sales:

Page Reads:

FREE:

Tuesday, 1/9

What to do:

Where to be:

Word count:

Sales:

Page Reads:

FREE:

Wednesday, 1/10

What to do:

Where to be:

Word count:

Sales:

Page Reads:

FREE:

January

Thursday, 1/11	Friday, 1/12	Saturday, 1/13	Sunday, 1/14
What to do:	**What to do:**	**What to do:**	**What to do:**
Where to be:	**Where to be:**	**Where to be:**	**Where to be:**
Word count:	**Word count:**	**Word count:**	**Word count:**
Sales: **Page Reads:** **FREE:**	**Sales:** **Page Reads:** **FREE:**	**Sales:** **Page Reads:** **FREE:**	**Sales:** **Page Reads:** **FREE:**

Week of

Goals

Weekly Checklist:

- [ ] Sign up for promos
- [ ] Change prices
- [ ] Order covers
- [ ] Schedule editor
- [ ] Complete edits
- [ ] Upload for sale
- [ ] Send ARCS
- [ ] Set up swaps
- [ ]

Monday, 1/15

What to do:

Where to be:

Word count:

Sales:

Page Reads:

FREE:

Tuesday, 1/16

What to do:

Where to be:

Word count:

Sales:

Page Reads:

FREE:

Wednesday, 1/17

What to do:

Where to be:

Word count:

Sales:

Page Reads:

FREE:

January

Thursday, 1/18

What to do:

Where to be:

Word count:

Sales:

Page Reads:

FREE:

Friday, 1/19

What to do:

Where to be:

Word count:

Sales:

Page Reads:

FREE:

Saturday, 1/20

What to do:

Where to be:

Word count:

Sales:

Page Reads:

FREE:

Sunday, 1/21

What to do:

Where to be:

Word count:

Sales:

Page Reads:

FREE:

 Week of

Goals

Weekly Checklist:

- [ ] Sign up for promos
- [ ] Change prices
- [ ] Order covers
- [ ] Schedule editor
- [ ] Complete edits
- [ ] Upload for sale
- [ ] Send ARCS
- [ ] Set up swaps
- [ ]

Monday, 1/22

What to do:

Where to be:

Word count:

Sales:

Page Reads:

FREE:

Tuesday, 1/23

What to do:

Where to be:

Word count:

Sales:

Page Reads:

FREE:

Wednesday, 1/24

What to do:

Where to be:

Word count:

Sales:

Page Reads:

FREE:

January

Thursday, 1/25

What to do:

Where to be:

Word count:

Sales:

Page Reads:

FREE:

Friday, 1/26

What to do:

Where to be:

Word count:

Sales:

Page Reads:

FREE:

Saturday, 1/27

What to do:

Where to be:

Word count:

Sales:

Page Reads:

FREE:

Sunday, 1/28

What to do:

Where to be:

Word count:

Sales:

Page Reads:

FREE:

Week of

Goals

Weekly Checklist:

- [ ] Sign up for promos
- [ ] Change prices
- [ ] Order covers
- [ ] Schedule editor
- [ ] Complete edits
- [ ] Upload for sale
- [ ] Send ARCS
- [ ] Set up swaps
- [ ]

Monday, 1/29

What to do:

Where to be:

Word count:

Sales:

Page Reads:

FREE:

Tuesday, 1/30

What to do:

Where to be:

Word count:

Sales:

Page Reads:

FREE:

Wednesday, 1/31

What to do:

Where to be:

Word count:

Sales:

Page Reads:

FREE:

February

Thursday, 2/1

What to do:

Where to be:

Word count:

Sales:

Page Reads:

FREE:

Friday, 2/2

What to do:

Where to be:

Word count:

Sales:

Page Reads:

FREE:

Saturday, 2/3

What to do:

Where to be:

Word count:

Sales:

Page Reads:

FREE:

Sunday, 2/4

What to do:

Where to be:

Word count:

Sales:

Page Reads:

FREE:

January Notes

What worked?

What changes do you need to make?

What new strategies will you try?

Notes:

Treat writing like a business

Here's my first tip:

Know your numbers.

Writing is an art. Making a living at it takes some business sense.

When I first started, I thought I could focus on the writing and the marketing would take care of itself. Yeah. I was wrong. In fact, I'm not sure I've ever been more wrong. See, this business, in a ridiculously saturated market, requires us to stay on top of things.

To get better, I joined groups, tried to see what other authors were doing to be successful. One of the first things I discovered was though I love words, numbers also have to be a big part of my life.

I did some analysis. While many people preach the dangers of going KU, I discovered that without a HUGE following, I was actually losing money by offering widespread distribution. The moment I started moving my books over to KU, my income improved. More recently, however, my income has increased dramatically.

What am I doing differently?

I'm treating my writing career like a business.

1. I record on a daily basis the number of page reads, FREE books, and sold books.

2. I know how much money to expect long before the report comes out on the 15th.

3. I keep a spreadsheet on Google Docs of all my expenses by the month.

4. Because I know how much I'm spending, I know how much I need to sell to be in the black. I spend differently when I consider how many books I have to sell to breakeven and turn a profit, how many reads I need.

5. I'm using KU to my advantage...and my newsletter. Yes, this is all about my Facebook Street Team, and my newsletter review team. I'm using my FREE days. (I'm detailing this in the course I'm creating.)

6. I've changed my attitude on FREE books. In the past, I never would've given away my books, but when I started the Firsts FREE for All and saw the jump in sales, I was encouraged. Now, I'm using these FREE days to increase my income, gain reviews, and find new readers.

So let's start by keeping track of all the important numbers related to your business: newsletter, Facebook page, Twitter, Instagram, Street Team, Review Team, book sales, free books, giveaways.

It doesn't have to be fancy. I use a Google Spreadsheet. No matter how you choose to do it, just know your numbers! This is how you know what works and what doesn't. This is how you know how to adjust, and where to focus your efforts for the biggest impact.

What I hope you'll discover is a way to adapt what I do to make it work for you. Maybe you'll find some strategies for earning more. I want everyone to be able to pay their bills while following their passion. No one decides to be an author because it's easy. This, like the army, is the toughest job I've ever loved.

February

Sunday	Monday	Tuesday	Wednesday	Thursday	Friday	Saturday
				1	2	3
4	5	6	7	8	9	10
11	12	13	14	15	16	17
18	19	20	21	22	23	24
25	26	27	28			

Week of

Goals

Weekly Checklist:
- [ ] Sign up for promos
- [ ] Change prices
- [ ] Order covers
- [ ] Schedule editor
- [ ] Complete edits
- [ ] Upload for sale
- [ ] Send ARCS
- [ ] Set up swaps
- [ ]

Monday, 2/5
What to do:

Where to be:

Word count:

Sales:

Page Reads:

FREE:

Tuesday, 2/6
What to do:

Where to be:

Word count:

Sales:

Page Reads:

FREE:

Wednesday, 2/7
What to do:

Where to be:

Word count:

Sales:

Page Reads:

FREE:

February

Thursday, 2/8

What to do:

Where to be:

Word count:

Sales:

Page Reads:

FREE:

Friday, 2/9

What to do:

Where to be:

Word count:

Sales:

Page Reads:

FREE:

Saturday, 2/10

What to do:

Where to be:

Word count:

Sales:

Page Reads:

FREE:

Sunday, 2/11

What to do:

Where to be:

Word count:

Sales:

Page Reads:

FREE:

Week of

Goals

Weekly Checklist:
- [ ] Sign up for promos
- [ ] Change prices
- [ ] Order covers
- [ ] Schedule editor
- [ ] Complete edits
- [ ] Upload for sale
- [ ] Send ARCS
- [ ] Set up swaps
- [ ]

Monday, 2/12
What to do:

Where to be:

Word count:

Sales:

Page Reads:

FREE:

Tuesday, 2/13
What to do:

Where to be:

Word count:

Sales:

Page Reads:

FREE:

Wednesday, 2/14
What to do:

Where to be:

Word count:

Sales:

Page Reads:

FREE:

February

Thursday, 2/15

What to do:

Where to be:

Word count:

Sales:
Page Reads:
FREE:

Friday, 2/16

What to do:

Where to be:

Word count:

Sales:
Page Reads:
FREE:

Saturday, 2/17

What to do:

Where to be:

Word count:

Sales:
Page Reads:
FREE:

Sunday, 2/18

What to do:

Where to be:

Word count:

Sales:
Page Reads:
FREE:

Week of

Goals

Weekly Checklist:
- [ ] Sign up for promos
- [ ] Change prices
- [ ] Order covers
- [ ] Schedule editor
- [ ] Complete edits
- [ ] Upload for sale
- [ ] Send ARCS
- [ ] Set up swaps
- [ ]

Monday, 2/19
What to do:

Where to be:

Word count:

Sales:

Page Reads:

FREE:

Tuesday, 2/20
What to do:

Where to be:

Word count:

Sales:

Page Reads:

FREE:

Wednesday, 2/21
What to do:

Where to be:

Word count:

Sales:

Page Reads:

FREE:

February

Thursday, 2/22 | Friday, 2/23 | Saturday, 2/24 | Sunday, 2/25

Thursday, 2/22	Friday, 2/23	Saturday, 2/24	Sunday, 2/25
What to do:	What to do:	What to do:	What to do:
Where to be:	Where to be:	Where to be:	Where to be:
Word count:	Word count:	Word count:	Word count:
Sales: Page Reads: FREE:	Sales: Page Reads: FREE:	Sales: Page Reads: FREE:	Sales: Page Reads: FREE:

Week of

Goals

Weekly Checklist:
- [ ] Sign up for promos
- [ ] Change prices
- [ ] Order covers
- [ ] Schedule editor
- [ ] Complete edits
- [ ] Upload for sale
- [ ] Send ARCS
- [ ] Set up swaps
- [ ]

Monday, 2/26
What to do:

Where to be:

Word count:

Sales:

Page Reads:

FREE:

Tuesday, 2/27
What to do:

Where to be:

Word count:

Sales:

Page Reads:

FREE:

Wednesday, 2/28
What to do:

Where to be:

Word count:

Sales:

Page Reads:

FREE:

March

Thursday, 3/1

What to do:

Where to be:

Word count:

Sales:
Page Reads:
FREE:

Friday, 3/2

What to do:

Where to be:

Word count:

Sales:
Page Reads:
FREE:

Saturday, 3/3

What to do:

Where to be:

Word count:

Sales:
Page Reads:
FREE:

Sunday, 3/4

What to do:

Where to be:

Word count:

Sales:
Page Reads:
FREE:

 # February Notes

What worked?

What changes do you need to make?

What new strategies will you try?

Notes:

 *March Pep Talk*

You're an author.

There's this unrelenting controversy in the book world. Way too many traditionally published authors seem to think Indie authors aren't *really* authors.

I don't care what anyone else says. Did you write a book? You're an author.

I've been with a publisher, not a big five, but a big boutique one. I hoped to expand my reach. Instead, I gave the owner marketing ideas, hoping she'd implement them on my books. She took those ideas, ran with them, and made herself a NYT bestseller.

Needless to say, I'm a bit soured on publishers who use me and take a hunk of my royalties without providing a real service.

I know plenty of traditionally published authors with big five publishers who don't earn nearly as much as I do. Insteaa, they work for slave wages and bragging rights.

This is why I started helping the Indie Community.

I created Love Kissed because I believe in Indies. We deserve to be able to earn a living doing what we love. I hoped to improve the community, teach authors how to build their careers.

Be proud. You're brave. You're innovative. You're determined. You're driven. You work hard. And no matter what anyone else says, you've earned your place on the shelves.

 # Last Month of the First Quarter!

If you're still doing everything on your own, you're working too hard!

Keep track of everything you do on a daily basis:

Keep track of everything you do when you release:

Which tasks can you hand off to a PA, an older kid, a spouse so you have more time to do what only you can do?

 March

Sunday	Monday	Tuesday	Wednesday	Thursday	Friday	Saturday
				1	2	3
4	5	6	7	8	9	10
11	12	13	14	15	16	17
18	19	20	21	22	23	24
25	26	27	28	29	30	31

Week of

Goals

Weekly Checklist:
- ☐ Sign up for promos
- ☐ Change prices
- ☐ Order covers
- ☐ Schedule editor
- ☐ Complete edits
- ☐ Upload for sale
- ☐ Send ARCS
- ☐ Set up swaps
- ☐

Monday, 3/5
What to do:

Where to be:

Word count:

Sales:

Page Reads:

FREE:

Tuesday, 3/6
What to do:

Where to be:

Word count:

Sales:

Page Reads:

FREE:

Wednesday, 3/7
What to do:

Where to be:

Word count:

Sales:

Page Reads:

FREE:

March

Thursday, 3/8

What to do:

Where to be:

Word count:

Sales:
Page Reads:
FREE:

Friday, 3/9

What to do:

Where to be:

Word count:

Sales:
Page Reads:
FREE:

Saturday, 3/10

What to do:

Where to be:

Word count:

Sales:
Page Reads:
FREE:

Sunday, 3/11

What to do:

Where to be:

Word count:

Sales:
Page Reads:
FREE:

Week of

Goals

Weekly Checklist:
- [ ] Sign up for promos
- [ ] Change prices
- [ ] Order covers
- [ ] Schedule editor
- [ ] Complete edits
- [ ] Upload for sale
- [ ] Send ARCS
- [ ] Set up swaps
- [ ]

Monday, 3/12
What to do:

Where to be:

Word count:

Sales:

Page Reads:

FREE:

Tuesday, 3/13
What to do:

Where to be:

Word count:

Sales:

Page Reads:

FREE:

Wednesday, 3/14
What to do:

Where to be:

Word count:

Sales:

Page Reads:

FREE:

March

Thursday, 3/15

What to do:

Where to be:

Word count:

Sales:
Page Reads:
FREE:

Friday, 3/16

What to do:

Where to be:

Word count:

Sales:
Page Reads:
FREE:

Saturday, 3/17

What to do:

Where to be:

Word count:

Sales:
Page Reads:
FREE:

Sunday, 3/18

What to do:

Where to be:

Word count:

Sales:
Page Reads:
FREE:

Week of

Goals

Weekly Checklist:
- [ ] Sign up for promos
- [ ] Change prices
- [ ] Order covers
- [ ] Schedule editor
- [ ] Complete edits
- [ ] Upload for sale
- [ ] Send ARCS
- [ ] Set up swaps
- [ ]

Monday, 3/19
What to do:

Where to be:

Word count:

Sales:

Page Reads:

FREE:

Tuesday, 3/20
What to do:

Where to be:

Word count:

Sales:

Page Reads:

FREE:

Wednesday, 3/21
What to do:

Where to be:

Word count:

Sales:

Page Reads:

FREE:

March

Thursday, 3/22

What to do:

Where to be:

Word count:

Sales:
Page Reads:
FREE:

Friday, 3/23

What to do:

Where to be:

Word count:

Sales:
Page Reads:
FREE:

Saturday, 3/24

What to do:

Where to be:

Word count:

Sales:
Page Reads:
FREE:

Sunday, 3/25

What to do:

Where to be:

Word count:

Sales:
Page Reads:
FREE:

Week of

Goals

Weekly Checklist:
- [ ] Sign up for promos
- [ ] Change prices
- [ ] Order covers
- [ ] Schedule editor
- [ ] Complete edits
- [ ] Upload for sale
- [ ] Send ARCS
- [ ] Set up swaps
- [ ]

Monday, 3/26
What to do:

Where to be:

Word count:

Sales:

Page Reads:

FREE:

Tuesday, 3/27
What to do:

Where to be:

Word count:

Sales:

Page Reads:

FREE:

Wednesday, 3/28
What to do:

Where to be:

Word count:

Sales:

Page Reads:

FREE:

March

Thursday, 3/29 | Friday, 3/30 | Saturday, 3/31 | Sunday, 4/1

What to do:

Where to be:

Word count:

Sales:

Page Reads:

FREE:

 # March Notes

What worked?

What changes do you need to make?

What new strategies will you try?

Notes:

April Pep Talk

Be the light. Be the change.

Let me begin by saying...this is a different kind of post, but I fully believe this too will have an impact on your career. See if you can follow my reasoning.

Shoot, I'm not even sure where to begin. I mean I could start with the past, the glorious golden age of the indie community when we were all rising to the top of the lists. Readers loved us, bloggers supported us, and we looked out for each other.

Through the years, the general sentiment around the community has changed. I know the reason for it: competition. The bubble burst. Suddenly, everyone could be an author. Tons of people tried. Some definitely should have. They wanted the career. They put in the work. They wrote their hearts out. They were part of what made the community so great.

Some just wanted to get rich quick and their efforts weakened the community. They published sub par work that shattered the respect we'd worked so hard to earn. They were so eager for success, they started using questionable marketing and promoting efforts that made everyone look bad. There have been plagiarism scandals. Piracy abounds. Authors started buying reviews instead of earning them. The competition for page reads has resulted in click farms. To make matters worse, Facebook changed their algorithms and had the nerve to want to make money. Amazon created KU. Our reach dwindled. The golden age turned yucky brass. (No offense to brass lovers, but brass will never be gold. Just saying.)

Those of us who have been around a while remember. We used to all be friends and support each other, but that has mostly stopped.

The truth is...we can never go back. We can't regain what we used to have, but we can move forward. We can create something better, stronger. We can be the light in times of darkness. We can be the change. How do we do this? For me, I make a concerted effort to be kind and considerate. Rather than force opinions down anyone's throat, I try to let my actions show who I am.

I don't claim to be some guru. I definitely don't know everything. What I am certain of, however, is that doing the right thing, striving each day to be a better person, better marketer, better author, to keep learning and sharing, and offering love and support has helped our little community grow. If you're a member of Love Kissed Author Promotions on Facebook, I can't tell you how much I appreciate what we're building, a place where we share, where there are no secrets or selfishness. If you're a romance author and you're not a member, what are you waiting for?

Being the light spills over into every aspect of the business. It helps me to attract the readers who'll love my books. It helps me attract the authors I love growing with. It helps my attitude, which is everything. Not every day is awesome, but I work hard to find the awesome in every day and hold onto it with both hands.

Let's keep it positive. Let's keep supporting one another. Let's be the best this community has to offer. And when you change your mindset, you'll find it changes your career in the most wondrous ways.

 # April

Sunday	Monday	Tuesday	Wednesday	Thursday	Friday	Saturday
1	2	3	4	5	6	7
8	9	10	11	12	13	14
15	16	17	18	19	20	21
22	23	24	25	26	27	28
29	30					

Week of

Goals

Weekly Checklist:

- ☐ Sign up for promos
- ☐ Change prices
- ☐ Order covers
- ☐ Schedule editor
- ☐ Complete edits
- ☐ Upload for sale
- ☐ Send ARCS
- ☐ Set up swaps
- ☐

Monday, 4/2

What to do:

Where to be:

Word count:

Sales:

Page Reads:

FREE:

Tuesday, 4/3

What to do:

Where to be:

Word count:

Sales:

Page Reads:

FREE:

Wednesday, 4/4

What to do:

Where to be:

Word count:

Sales:

Page Reads:

FREE:

April

Thursday, 4/5

What to do:

Where to be:

Word count:

Sales:
Page Reads:
FREE:

Friday, 4/6

What to do:

Where to be:

Word count:

Sales:
Page Reads:
FREE:

Saturday, 4/7

What to do:

Where to be:

Word count:

Sales:
Page Reads:
FREE:

Sunday, 4/8

What to do:

Where to be:

Word count:

Sales:
Page Reads:
FREE:

Week of

Goals

Weekly Checklist:
- ☐ Sign up for promos
- ☐ Change prices
- ☐ Order covers
- ☐ Schedule editor
- ☐ Complete edits
- ☐ Upload for sale
- ☐ Send ARCS
- ☐ Set up swaps
- ☐

Monday, 4/9
What to do:

Where to be:

Word count:

Sales:

Page Reads:

FREE:

Tuesday, 4/10
What to do:

Where to be:

Word count:

Sales:

Page Reads:

FREE:

Wednesday, 4/11
What to do:

Where to be:

Word count:

Sales:

Page Reads:

FREE:

April

Thursday, 4/12

What to do:

Where to be:

Word count:

Sales:

Page Reads:

FREE:

Friday, 4/13

What to do:

Where to be:

Word count:

Sales:

Page Reads:

FREE:

Saturday, 4/14

What to do:

Where to be:

Word count:

Sales:

Page Reads:

FREE:

Sunday, 4/15

What to do:

Where to be:

Word count:

Sales:

Page Reads:

FREE:

Week of

Goals	Monday, 4/16	Tuesday, 4/17	Wednesday, 4/18
	What to do:	What to do:	What to do:
	Where to be:	Where to be:	Where to be:
	Word count:	Word count:	Word count:
	Sales: Page Reads: FREE:	Sales: Page Reads: FREE:	Sales: Page Reads: FREE:

Weekly Checklist:

- ☐ Sign up for promos
- ☐ Change prices
- ☐ Order covers
- ☐ Schedule editor
- ☐ Complete edits
- ☐ Upload for sale
- ☐ Send ARCS
- ☐ Set up swaps
- ☐

April

Thursday, 4/19

What to do:

Where to be:

Word count:

Sales:

Page Reads:

FREE:

Friday, 4/20

What to do:

Where to be:

Word count:

Sales:

Page Reads:

FREE:

Saturday, 4/21

What to do:

Where to be:

Word count:

Sales:

Page Reads:

FREE:

Sunday, 4/22

What to do:

Where to be:

Word count:

Sales:

Page Reads:

FREE:

Week of

Goals

Weekly Checklist:

- [ ] Sign up for promos
- [ ] Change prices
- [ ] Order covers
- [ ] Schedule editor
- [ ] Complete edits
- [ ] Upload for sale
- [ ] Send ARCS
- [ ] Set up swaps
- [ ]

Monday, 4/23

What to do:

Where to be:

Word count:

Sales:

Page Reads:

FREE:

Tuesday, 4/24

What to do:

Where to be:

Word count:

Sales:

Page Reads:

FREE:

Wednesday, 4/25

What to do:

Where to be:

Word count:

Sales:

Page Reads:

FREE:

April

Thursday, 4/26

What to do:

Where to be:

Word count:

Sales:

Page Reads:

FREE:

Friday, 4/27

What to do:

Where to be:

Word count:

Sales:

Page Reads:

FREE:

Saturday, 4/28

What to do:

Where to be:

Word count:

Sales:

Page Reads:

FREE:

Sunday, 4/29

What to do:

Where to be:

Word count:

Sales:

Page Reads:

FREE:

 # April Notes

What worked?

What changes do you need to make?

What new strategies will you try?

Notes:

Your list is the lifeblood of your career.

Let me tell you a story. Ready?

Once upon a time, there was an author who thought writing a great book was enough. She would write her heart out and publish nearly every month. At first, she was right! There wasn't a lot of competition on Amazon or any of the other sites. She published wide and made a really good living.

Unfortunately, the author was very short sighted and didn't consider how much self-publishing and social media would change over time. Suddenly, there was a huge influx of new authors whose dreams of fame and fortune had been bolstered by the recent indie success. The market was flooded. Ah, but she still did *okay* by sharing on her Facebook page. Then the powers that be changed the algorithms and wanted authors to pay for advertising.

This was the final nail in the coffin holding her career. She toyed with quitting, but ever since she was little, being an author had been her big dream, writing was her happy place, and the idea of earning a living doing anything else seemed like a half life at best. So, she made a vow to treat her chosen career as a business in 2016.

The author made a concerted effort to grow her list, and marketing lists. She had always been much better at promoting others than she had been at promoting herself. She decided to take a leap...and the net appeared. Her piddly list grew. It grew and it grew and it grew. She learned how to use that list to her advantage. Her book sales grew, her page reads grew, her income grew.

Other authors started asking her about the secret of her newfound success. *whispers* *It's the list.*

Grow your lists like your life depends on it...because it really does.

You want to make a living as an author? It's not all about writing being an art form. It's a business too.

What's the list for?

It's your first and best mode of marketing.

How do I grow my list?

Through giveaways.

Why would you do it that way? Don't you get a lot of unsubscribes?

Me? No. I don't. I make sure when I send an email, it has value. They signed up through a giveaway, and I participate in a lot of giveaways. So, I share more giveaways. I share my FREE books. And I offer opportunities to join my review team and street team. Hardly anyone unsubscribes. Even better, I take people who started liking me to win something, and turn them into loyal readers. They read and review. It helps me grow. It's a nice symbiotic relationship we have going on.

So grow those lists. Create rabid readers. Give your career a helping hand.

 *May*

Sunday	Monday	Tuesday	Wednesday	Thursday	Friday	Saturday
		1	2	3	4	5
6	7	8	9	10	11	12
13	14	15	16	17	18	19
20	21	22	23	24	25	26
27	28	29	30	31		

Week of

Goals

Weekly Checklist:

- ☐ Sign up for promos
- ☐ Change prices
- ☐ Order covers
- ☐ Schedule editor
- ☐ Complete edits
- ☐ Upload for sale
- ☐ Send ARCS
- ☐ Set up swaps
- ☐

Monday, 4/30

What to do:

Where to be:

Word count:

Sales:

Page Reads:

FREE:

Tuesday, 5/1

What to do:

Where to be:

Word count:

Sales:

Page Reads:

FREE:

Wednesday, 5/2

What to do:

Where to be:

Word count:

Sales:

Page Reads:

FREE:

May

Thursday, 5/3

What to do:

Where to be:

Word count:

Sales:
Page Reads:
FREE:

Friday, 5/4

What to do:

Where to be:

Word count:

Sales:
Page Reads:
FREE:

Saturday, 5/5

What to do:

Where to be:

Word count:

Sales:
Page Reads:
FREE:

Sunday, 5/6

What to do:

Where to be:

Word count:

Sales:
Page Reads:
FREE:

Week of

Goals

Weekly Checklist:
- ☐ Sign up for promos
- ☐ Change prices
- ☐ Order covers
- ☐ Schedule editor
- ☐ Complete edits
- ☐ Upload for sale
- ☐ Send ARCS
- ☐ Set up swaps
- ☐

Monday, 5/7
What to do:

Where to be:

Word count:

Sales:

Page Reads:

FREE:

Tuesday, 5/8
What to do:

Where to be:

Word count:

Sales:

Page Reads:

FREE:

Wednesday, 5/9
What to do:

Where to be:

Word count:

Sales:

Page Reads:

FREE:

May

Thursday, 5/10 | Friday, 5/11 | Saturday, 5/12 | Sunday, 5/13

What to do:

Where to be:

Word count:

Sales:

Page Reads:

FREE:

Week of

Goals

Weekly Checklist:
- [ ] Sign up for promos
- [ ] Change prices
- [ ] Order covers
- [ ] Schedule editor
- [ ] Complete edits
- [ ] Upload for sale
- [ ] Send ARCS
- [ ] Set up swaps
- [ ]

Monday, 5/14
What to do:

Where to be:

Word count:

Sales:

Page Reads:

FREE:

Tuesday, 5/15
What to do:

Where to be:

Word count:

Sales:

Page Reads:

FREE:

Wednesday, 5/16
What to do:

Where to be:

Word count:

Sales:

Page Reads:

FREE:

May

Thursday, 5/17

What to do:

Where to be:

Word count:

Sales:
Page Reads:
FREE:

Friday, 5/18

What to do:

Where to be:

Word count:

Sales:
Page Reads:
FREE:

Saturday, 5/19

What to do:

Where to be:

Word count:

Sales:
Page Reads:
FREE:

Sunday, 5/20

What to do:

Where to be:

Word count:

Sales:
Page Reads:
FREE:

Week of

Goals

Weekly Checklist:
- [ ] Sign up for promos
- [ ] Change prices
- [ ] Order covers
- [ ] Schedule editor
- [ ] Complete edits
- [ ] Upload for sale
- [ ] Send ARCS
- [ ] Set up swaps
- [ ]

Monday, 5/21

What to do:

Where to be:

Word count:

Sales:

Page Reads:

FREE:

Tuesday, 5/22

What to do:

Where to be:

Word count:

Sales:

Page Reads:

FREE:

Wednesday, 5/23

What to do:

Where to be:

Word count:

Sales:

Page Reads:

FREE:

May

Thursday, 5/24

What to do:

Where to be:

Word count:

Sales:
Page Reads:
FREE:

Friday, 5/25

What to do:

Where to be:

Word count:

Sales:
Page Reads:
FREE:

Saturday, 5/26

What to do:

Where to be:

Word count:

Sales:
Page Reads:
FREE:

Sunday, 5/27

What to do:

Where to be:

Word count:

Sales:
Page Reads:
FREE:

Week of

Goals

Weekly Checklist:
- [ ] Sign up for promos
- [ ] Change prices
- [ ] Order covers
- [ ] Schedule editor
- [ ] Complete edits
- [ ] Upload for sale
- [ ] Send ARCS
- [ ] Set up swaps
- [ ]

Monday, 5/28

What to do:

Where to be:

Word count:

Sales:

Page Reads:

FREE:

Tuesday, 5/29

What to do:

Where to be:

Word count:

Sales:

Page Reads:

FREE:

Wednesday, 5/30

What to do:

Where to be:

Word count:

Sales:

Page Reads:

FREE:

June

Thursday, 5/31

What to do:

Where to be:

Word count:

Sales:
Page Reads:
FREE:

Friday, 6/1

What to do:

Where to be:

Word count:

Sales:
Page Reads:
FREE:

Saturday, 6/2

What to do:

Where to be:

Word count:

Sales:
Page Reads:
FREE:

Sunday, 6/3

What to do:

Where to be:

Word count:

Sales:
Page Reads:
FREE:

 May Notes

What worked?

What changes do you need to make?

What new strategies will you try?

Notes:

My theory on List Building Giveaways

1. *Do they work?*

Yes. The goal is to get some emails. Bam. You've got emails!

2. *Are they worth it if I get a bunch of unsubscribes?*

Yes. Those who unsubscribe are people you don't have to pay for. Now, if you have too many unsubscribes you may need to reconsider your follow up strategy.

This brings us to...

3. *How to keep them & convert them:*

Keep in mind your readers are bombarded with newsletters. Seriously. In these list giveaways, they add probably at least 40 other authors at the same time. It can be overwhelming. If you don't grab their interest and attention, they're going to fall off.

It's a combination of things.

a. *Is your newsletter pretty?*

Make it pretty. Be the good looking chick everyone wants to dance with.

b. *Know your audience.*

These readers signed up for a giveaway. Chances are, they want free stuff. They want giveaways. They don't want to be sold. You have to earn that right. I mean it. They can unsubscribe as quickly as they signed up.

Build the relationship with them. Do you want someone to walk up to you and ask you to hop into bed with them? Whoa! Too. Soon. This is what you're doing when you try to sell them before you've earned it. Think of the three date rule. Better yet, let them take the lead. Most of the people who sign up have no idea who you are. After all, they didn't sign up just for you out of the blue; they entered to win a giveaway. They didn't win. They may want to go find a new giveaway. Others may want to stick around and check you out.

Here's what's working for me:

After I add the list, I send an opportunity newsletter. Nothing fancy.

https://madmimi.com/s/3c23a8

Do I get unsubscribes? *Yes.* Do I sweat it? *No.* It's like dating. Not all the relationships are going to work out. You don't need a ton. You need the one special one. Find your avid readers who become your rabid fans. They will do anything they can to help you grow.

So, I send the newsletter then...

I sit back and watch my numbers grow. Each week I offer FREE books to those in the review/street team. I only share big FREEBIES & giveaways with my newsletter. I build a relationship with those who want one and those who stick around for the goodies get those too. Everyone gets the opportunity newsletter again when I add people. Why? People change their mind. Maybe they actually read it this time. Maybe they've seen your name enough that you have brand recognition. It builds trust. Don't break it.

Create a nice, and ultimately profitable relationship.

Clearly it's working because of these things: my increased income from page reads and sales, my growing groups, and the feedback from members. They ask if they can invite their friends. They talk about the group at IRL gatherings. (So weird, in a wonderful way.) They can't wait for the rest of the series to be free so they buy the boxed set and then rave about it.

Be patient. Do the work. Reap the rewards.

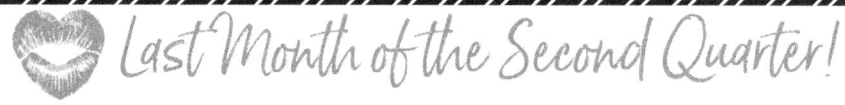 # Last Month of the Second Quarter!

Summer can be slow for sales.

What can you do to boost your visibility?

Are you monitoring your expenses to ensure you stay in the black?

What can you do to put yourself in place for a fantastic fall?

 *June*

Sunday	Monday	Tuesday	Wednesday	Thursday	Friday	Saturday
					1	2
3	4	5	6	7	8	9
10	11	12	13	14	15	16
17	18	19	20	21	22	23
24	25	26	27	28	29	30

Week of

Goals

Weekly Checklist:
- ☐ Sign up for promos
- ☐ Change prices
- ☐ Order covers
- ☐ Schedule editor
- ☐ Complete edits
- ☐ Upload for sale
- ☐ Send ARCS
- ☐ Set up swaps
- ☐

Monday, 6/4
What to do:

Where to be:

Word count:

Sales:

Page Reads:

FREE:

Tuesday, 6/5
What to do:

Where to be:

Word count:

Sales:

Page Reads:

FREE:

Wednesday, 6/6
What to do:

Where to be:

Word count:

Sales:

Page Reads:

FREE:

June

Thursday, 6/7 | Friday, 6/8 | Saturday, 6/9 | Sunday, 6/10

What to do:

Where to be:

Word count:

Sales:
Page Reads:
FREE:

Week of

Goals

Weekly Checklist:

- ☐ Sign up for promos
- ☐ Change prices
- ☐ Order covers
- ☐ Schedule editor
- ☐ Complete edits
- ☐ Upload for sale
- ☐ Send ARCS
- ☐ Set up swaps
- ☐

Monday, 6/11

What to do:

Where to be:

Word count:

Sales:

Page Reads:

FREE:

Tuesday, 6/12

What to do:

Where to be:

Word count:

Sales:

Page Reads:

FREE:

Wednesday, 6/13

What to do:

Where to be:

Word count:

Sales:

Page Reads:

FREE:

June

Thursday, 6/14

What to do:

Where to be:

Word count:

Sales:

Page Reads:

FREE:

Friday, 6/15

What to do:

Where to be:

Word count:

Sales:

Page Reads:

FREE:

Saturday, 6/16

What to do:

Where to be:

Word count:

Sales:

Page Reads:

FREE:

Sunday, 6/17

What to do:

Where to be:

Word count:

Sales:

Page Reads:

FREE:

Week of

Goals

Weekly Checklist:

- ☐ Sign up for promos
- ☐ Change prices
- ☐ Order covers
- ☐ Schedule editor
- ☐ Complete edits
- ☐ Upload for sale
- ☐ Send ARCS
- ☐ Set up swaps
- ☐

Monday, 6/18

What to do:

Where to be:

Word count:

Sales:

Page Reads:

FREE:

Tuesday, 6/19

What to do:

Where to be:

Word count:

Sales:

Page Reads:

FREE:

Wednesday, 6/20

What to do:

Where to be:

Word count:

Sales:

Page Reads:

FREE:

June

Thursday, 6/21

What to do:

Where to be:

Word count:

Sales:
Page Reads:
FREE:

Friday, 6/22

What to do:

Where to be:

Word count:

Sales:
Page Reads:
FREE:

Saturday, 6/23

What to do:

Where to be:

Word count:

Sales:
Page Reads:
FREE:

Sunday, 6/24

What to do:

Where to be:

Word count:

Sales:
Page Reads:
FREE:

Week of

Goals

Weekly Checklist:
- ☐ Sign up for promos
- ☐ Change prices
- ☐ Order covers
- ☐ Schedule editor
- ☐ Complete edits
- ☐ Upload for sale
- ☐ Send ARCS
- ☐ Set up swaps
- ☐

Monday, 6/25
What to do:

Where to be:

Word count:

Sales:

Page Reads:

FREE:

Tuesday, 6/26
What to do:

Where to be:

Word count:

Sales:

Page Reads:

FREE:

Wednesday, 6/27
What to do:

Where to be:

Word count:

Sales:

Page Reads:

FREE:

June

Thursday, 6/28

What to do:

Where to be:

Word count:

Sales:
Page Reads:
FREE:

Friday, 6/29

What to do:

Where to be:

Word count:

Sales:
Page Reads:
FREE:

Saturday, 6/30

What to do:

Where to be:

Word count:

Sales:
Page Reads:
FREE:

Sunday, 7/1

What to do:

Where to be:

Word count:

Sales:
Page Reads:
FREE:

 June Notes

What worked?

What changes do you need to make?

What new strategies will you try?

Notes:

 July Pep Talk

Change your mindset, change your life.

Today, I plan to wax philosophical for a moment. That was your warning.

I've been speaking with a lot of authors lately. I get PMs. They are awesome. I'm glad you find me approachable and reach out. More than anything, I want to help.

In this industry, practically nothing comes easily. There's nothing easy about writing a book, or finding a great editor, or discovering betas who will stick with you, or creating the perfect cover...the list is endless. You get the idea. You know it. You live it.

Still, I find there's one thing that comes waaaaaay too easily: getting discouraged.

Seriously. Being an author means waking up every day and washing your thick skin before putting on your big girl panties. It's hard, yo. 😉

Or it can feel hard. To survive, we need to retrain our mind. Got it?

Step 1: *Where you once saw obstacles, see opportunities.*

Make it your mantra. Repeat after me: Where others see obstacles, I see opportunities. Okay. Now say it again. Keep saying it until you believe it. And instead of getting frustrated and shutting down, move on to step two.

Step 2: *Become a master of problem solving.*

I was asked yesterday by one of our authors how I ended up doing all this. After an incredibly long story she ever so patiently waded through, I realized I should've simply told her about seeing opportunities.

This is how I create so many of our Love Kissed Book Bargains promotions. Yesterday, I could've been frustrated about the challenges of FREE book promotions and the impact on an Amazon Associate account, resulting in lost earning. Instead, I thought about it, did some research, and found a way to still help authors promote free books while protecting one income stream.

Life is full of challenges, but it's also full of promise. Want success? There's no magical formula. Okay, maybe step three...

Step 3: *Lather, rinse, repeat. Just keep swimming. Keep on keeping on.*

Whatever your favorite little catch phrase is, whatever pulls you through.

Seek out the opportunities in your life. Practice positivity. If you change your attitude, you change your life.

 *July*

Sunday	Monday	Tuesday	Wednesday	Thursday	Friday	Saturday
1	2	3	4	5	6	7
8	9	10	11	12	13	14
15	16	17	18	19	20	21
22	23	24	25	26	27	28
29	30	31				

Week of

Goals

Weekly Checklist:
- [ ] Sign up for promos
- [ ] Change prices
- [ ] Order covers
- [ ] Schedule editor
- [ ] Complete edits
- [ ] Upload for sale
- [ ] Send ARCS
- [ ] Set up swaps
- [ ]

Monday, 7/2
What to do:

Where to be:

Word count:

Sales:

Page Reads:

FREE:

Tuesday, 7/3
What to do:

Where to be:

Word count:

Sales:

Page Reads:

FREE:

Wednesday, 7/4
What to do:

Where to be:

Word count:

Sales:

Page Reads:

FREE:

July

Thursday, 7/5 | Friday, 7/6 | Saturday, 7/7 | Sunday, 7/8

What to do:

Where to be:

Word count:

Sales:
Page Reads:
FREE:

Week of

Goals

Weekly Checklist:

- ☐ Sign up for promos
- ☐ Change prices
- ☐ Order covers
- ☐ Schedule editor
- ☐ Complete edits
- ☐ Upload for sale
- ☐ Send ARCS
- ☐ Set up swaps
- ☐

Monday, 7/9

What to do:

Where to be:

Word count:

Sales:

Page Reads:

FREE:

Tuesday, 7/10

What to do:

Where to be:

Word count:

Sales:

Page Reads:

FREE:

Wednesday, 7/11

What to do:

Where to be:

Word count:

Sales:

Page Reads:

FREE:

July

Thursday, 7/12

What to do:

Where to be:

Word count:

Sales:
Page Reads:
FREE:

Friday, 7/13

What to do:

Where to be:

Word count:

Sales:
Page Reads:
FREE:

Saturday, 7/14

What to do:

Where to be:

Word count:

Sales:
Page Reads:
FREE:

Sunday, 7/15

What to do:

Where to be:

Word count:

Sales:
Page Reads:
FREE:

Week of

Goals

Weekly Checklist:
- [ ] Sign up for promos
- [ ] Change prices
- [ ] Order covers
- [ ] Schedule editor
- [ ] Complete edits
- [ ] Upload for sale
- [ ] Send ARCS
- [ ] Set up swaps
- [ ]

Monday, 7/16
What to do:

Where to be:

Word count:

Sales:

Page Reads:

FREE:

Tuesday, 7/17
What to do:

Where to be:

Word count:

Sales:

Page Reads:

FREE:

Wednesday, 7/18
What to do:

Where to be:

Word count:

Sales:

Page Reads:

FREE:

July

Thursday, 7/19

What to do:

Where to be:

Word count:

Sales:
Page Reads:
FREE:

Friday, 7/20

What to do:

Where to be:

Word count:

Sales:
Page Reads:
FREE:

Saturday, 7/21

What to do:

Where to be:

Word count:

Sales:
Page Reads:
FREE:

Sunday, 7/22

What to do:

Where to be:

Word count:

Sales:
Page Reads:
FREE:

Week of

Goals

Weekly Checklist:
- ☐ Sign up for promos
- ☐ Change prices
- ☐ Order covers
- ☐ Schedule editor
- ☐ Complete edits
- ☐ Upload for sale
- ☐ Send ARCS
- ☐ Set up swaps
- ☐

Monday, 7/23
What to do:

Where to be:

Word count:

Sales:

Page Reads:

FREE:

Tuesday, 7/24
What to do:

Where to be:

Word count:

Sales:

Page Reads:

FREE:

Wednesday, 7/25
What to do:

Where to be:

Word count:

Sales:

Page Reads:

FREE:

July

Thursday, 7/26

What to do:

Where to be:

Word count:

Sales:
Page Reads:
FREE:

Friday, 7/27

What to do:

Where to be:

Word count:

Sales:
Page Reads:
FREE:

Saturday, 7/28

What to do:

Where to be:

Word count:

Sales:
Page Reads:
FREE:

Sunday, 7/29

What to do:

Where to be:

Word count:

Sales:
Page Reads:
FREE:

What worked?

What changes do you need to make?

What new strategies will you try?

Notes:

Building a Life You Love

Remember one of our last pep talks? Change your mindset and change your life? It's a process. Practice this every day.

Take a moment and recall why you started writing. This needs to be your passion. You have to feel like you'll be incomplete if you don't write. Crafting plots has to be something you love. Finding the perfect words to express your thoughts must be something you're driven to do.

This isn't a get rich quick kinda career. It can be incredibly lonely. Worse, sometimes you make friends and discover you've only been frenemies all along. It's easy to feel isolated and alone, worried over who you can truly trust.

Been there. Done that. Lots of times.

Not only is it disheartening and completely debilitating, but suddenly there's a crack in your thick skin that leaves you wide open for doubt to come creeping in. ☺

Ready for some good news? When you feel broken, remember: that's how the light gets in. Find those people in your life who make you feel whole again. Find people who remind you that you're talented.

Because you are. You're talented. You're smart. You're important. Be kind...to others and yourself. Dust yourself off. I promise you that after the dark, when the light seeps in, life doesn't seem so hard anymore.

You want to sell 15 books a day? You can. You will.

You want to be able to stay home and write full time? You can. You will.

Whether you believe you'll fail or you'll succeed...you will. Stay positive. Sometimes your efforts produce results, and sometimes you learn.

This is summer. Still. Soon it will be fall, a huge season for us. I've spent all summer testing new theories, positioning myself for success and leaping. Guess what? The net appeared.

Want the secret of my success? In the Love Kissed Books Author Group on Facebook, I built a place for me (and everyone to flourish). I try to fill our little community with positivity because the negativity is so easy to come by. In the Indie community, there will always be people who try to cut you down because it makes them feel bigger. Shake it off. Find your people. Focus on your career. Be the light.

Build a life you love. Spread love. Watch how much everything changes.

August

Sunday	Monday	Tuesday	Wednesday	Thursday	Friday	Saturday
			1	2	3	4
5	6	7	8	9	10	11
12	13	14	15	16	17	18
19	20	21	22	23	24	25
26	27	28	29	30	31	

Week of

Goals

Weekly Checklist:
- [ ] Sign up for promos
- [ ] Change prices
- [ ] Order covers
- [ ] Schedule editor
- [ ] Complete edits
- [ ] Upload for sale
- [ ] Send ARCS
- [ ] Set up swaps
- [ ]

Monday, 7/30
What to do:

Where to be:

Word count:

Sales:

Page Reads:

FREE:

Tuesday, 7/31
What to do:

Where to be:

Word count:

Sales:

Page Reads:

FREE:

Wednesday, 8/1
What to do:

Where to be:

Word count:

Sales:

Page Reads:

FREE:

August

Thursday, 8/2

What to do:

Where to be:

Word count:

Sales:
Page Reads:
FREE:

Friday, 8/3

What to do:

Where to be:

Word count:

Sales:
Page Reads:
FREE:

Saturday, 8/4

What to do:

Where to be:

Word count:

Sales:
Page Reads:
FREE:

Sunday, 8/5

What to do:

Where to be:

Word count:

Sales:
Page Reads:
FREE:

Week of

Goals

Weekly Checklist:
- ☐ Sign up for promos
- ☐ Change prices
- ☐ Order covers
- ☐ Schedule editor
- ☐ Complete edits
- ☐ Upload for sale
- ☐ Send ARCS
- ☐ Set up swaps
- ☐

Monday, 8/6
What to do:

Where to be:

Word count:

Sales:

Page Reads:

FREE:

Tuesday, 8/7
What to do:

Where to be:

Word count:

Sales:

Page Reads:

FREE:

Wednesday, 8/8
What to do:

Where to be:

Word count:

Sales:

Page Reads:

FREE:

August

Thursday, 8/9

What to do:

Where to be:

Word count:

Sales:

Page Reads:

FREE:

Friday, 8/10

What to do:

Where to be:

Word count:

Sales:

Page Reads:

FREE:

Saturday, 8/11

What to do:

Where to be:

Word count:

Sales:

Page Reads:

FREE:

Sunday, 8/12

What to do:

Where to be:

Word count:

Sales:

Page Reads:

FREE:

Week of

Goals

Weekly Checklist:
- [ ] Sign up for promos
- [ ] Change prices
- [ ] Order covers
- [ ] Schedule editor
- [ ] Complete edits
- [ ] Upload for sale
- [ ] Send ARCS
- [ ] Set up swaps
- [ ]

Monday, 8/13
What to do:

Where to be:

Word count:

Sales:

Page Reads:

FREE:

Tuesday, 8/14
What to do:

Where to be:

Word count:

Sales:

Page Reads:

FREE:

Wednesday, 8/15
What to do:

Where to be:

Word count:

Sales:

Page Reads:

FREE:

August

Thursday, 8/16 | Friday, 8/17 | Saturday, 8/18 | Sunday, 8/19

What to do:

Where to be:

Word count:

Sales:

Page Reads:

FREE:

Week of

Goals

Weekly Checklist:
- [ ] Sign up for promos
- [ ] Change prices
- [ ] Order covers
- [ ] Schedule editor
- [ ] Complete edits
- [ ] Upload for sale
- [ ] Send ARCS
- [ ] Set up swaps
- [ ]

Monday, 8/20
What to do:

Where to be:

Word count:

Sales:

Page Reads:

FREE:

Tuesday, 8/21
What to do:

Where to be:

Word count:

Sales:

Page Reads:

FREE:

Wednesday, 8/22
What to do:

Where to be:

Word count:

Sales:

Page Reads:

FREE:

August

Thursday, 8/23

What to do:

Where to be:

Word count:

Sales:
Page Reads:
FREE:

Friday, 8/24

What to do:

Where to be:

Word count:

Sales:
Page Reads:
FREE:

Saturday, 8/25

What to do:

Where to be:

Word count:

Sales:
Page Reads:
FREE:

Sunday, 8/26

What to do:

Where to be:

Word count:

Sales:
Page Reads:
FREE:

Week of

Goals

Weekly Checklist:

- ☐ Sign up for promos
- ☐ Change prices
- ☐ Order covers
- ☐ Schedule editor
- ☐ Complete edits
- ☐ Upload for sale
- ☐ Send ARCS
- ☐ Set up swaps
- ☐

Monday, 8/27

What to do:

Where to be:

Word count:

Sales:

Page Reads:

FREE:

Tuesday, 8/28

What to do:

Where to be:

Word count:

Sales:

Page Reads:

FREE:

Wednesday, 8/29

What to do:

Where to be:

Word count:

Sales:

Page Reads:

FREE:

August

Thursday, 8/30

What to do:

Where to be:

Word count:

Sales:
Page Reads:
FREE:

Friday, 8/31

What to do:

Where to be:

Word count:

Sales:
Page Reads:
FREE:

Saturday, 9/1

What to do:

Where to be:

Word count:

Sales:
Page Reads:
FREE:

Sunday, 9/2

What to do:

Where to be:

Word count:

Sales:
Page Reads:
FREE:

 # August Notes

What worked?

What changes do you need to make?

What new strategies will you try?

Notes:

 *September Pep Talk*

We're not in competition.

Okay. *takes a deep breath* I was in another author marketing group. I like to see what others are sharing because if I can help all of us to be better, I'm gonna do it. I was that philosophical teen who read Khalil Gibran and had posters of quotes instead of hot guys. I still am. (Not the teen part. Stay with me. I'm being philosophical.) And I practice what I believe. I believe in giving. I believe in sharing. I believe we're all better for living a life of love.

Anyway, I'm reading through these group posts and this woman is preaching to her group that other authors are your competition. I don't believe that. Sorry. I don't. That philosophy only implies that if someone else wins, I lose. Based on Amazon sales, that's crap. Yeah, I said it. No one buys just one book. It's like nobody eats only one potato chip. She doesn't think authors should be your Twitter followers. She doesn't think other authors will help you sell books. Okay, maybe if they have that attitude, they won't.

I think we can prove this group and author wrong. I believe that other authors should be our biggest cheerleaders. After all, only another author understands what a feat it is to publish, to hit a list, to make top 100. I promise, if I see a post where something awesome happened with your publishing career, I'll be there cheering you on. Your success takes nothing from me. It only encourages me.

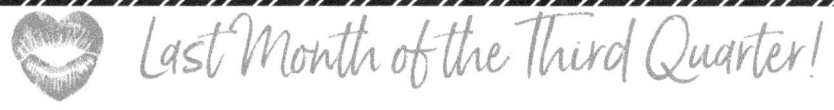 

Last Month of the Third Quarter!

Fall is awesome for sales!

Have you planned your fall release(s)?

Have you planned to promote your backlist?

What can you do to make this your strongest quarter yet?

September

Sunday	Monday	Tuesday	Wednesday	Thursday	Friday	Saturday
						1
2	3	4	5	6	7	8
9	10	11	12	13	14	15
16	17	18	19	20	21	22
23/30	24	25	26	27	28	29

Week of

Goals

Weekly Checklist:
- ☐ Sign up for promos
- ☐ Change prices
- ☐ Order covers
- ☐ Schedule editor
- ☐ Complete edits
- ☐ Upload for sale
- ☐ Send ARCS
- ☐ Set up swaps
- ☐

Monday, 9/3
What to do:

Where to be:

Word count:

Sales:

Page Reads:

FREE:

Tuesday, 9/4
What to do:

Where to be:

Word count:

Sales:

Page Reads:

FREE:

Wednesday, 9/5
What to do:

Where to be:

Word count:

Sales:

Page Reads:

FREE:

September

Thursday, 9/6

What to do:

Where to be:

Word count:

Sales:

Page Reads:

FREE:

Friday, 9/7

What to do:

Where to be:

Word count:

Sales:

Page Reads:

FREE:

Saturday, 9/8

What to do:

Where to be:

Word count:

Sales:

Page Reads:

FREE:

Sunday, 9/9

What to do:

Where to be:

Word count:

Sales:

Page Reads:

FREE:

Week of

Goals

Weekly Checklist:

- [ ] Sign up for promos
- [ ] Change prices
- [ ] Order covers
- [ ] Schedule editor
- [ ] Complete edits
- [ ] Upload for sale
- [ ] Send ARCS
- [ ] Set up swaps
- [ ]

Monday, 9/10

What to do:

Where to be:

Word count:

Sales:

Page Reads:

FREE:

Tuesday, 9/11

What to do:

Where to be:

Word count:

Sales:

Page Reads:

FREE:

Wednesday, 9/12

What to do:

Where to be:

Word count:

Sales:

Page Reads:

FREE:

September

Thursday, 9/13

What to do:

Where to be:

Word count:

Sales:
Page Reads:
FREE:

Friday, 9/14

What to do:

Where to be:

Word count:

Sales:
Page Reads:
FREE:

Saturday, 9/15

What to do:

Where to be:

Word count:

Sales:
Page Reads:
FREE:

Sunday, 9/16

What to do:

Where to be:

Word count:

Sales:
Page Reads:
FREE:

Week of

Goals

Weekly Checklist:

- ☐ Sign up for promos
- ☐ Change prices
- ☐ Order covers
- ☐ Schedule editor
- ☐ Complete edits
- ☐ Upload for sale
- ☐ Send ARCS
- ☐ Set up swaps
- ☐

Monday, 9/17

What to do:

Where to be:

Word count:

Sales:

Page Reads:

FREE:

Tuesday, 9/18

What to do:

Where to be:

Word count:

Sales:

Page Reads:

FREE:

Wednesday, 9/19

What to do:

Where to be:

Word count:

Sales:

Page Reads:

FREE:

September

Thursday, 9/20

What to do:

Where to be:

Word count:

Sales:
Page Reads:
FREE:

Friday, 9/21

What to do:

Where to be:

Word count:

Sales:
Page Reads:
FREE:

Saturday, 9/22

What to do:

Where to be:

Word count:

Sales:
Page Reads:
FREE:

Sunday, 9/23

What to do:

Where to be:

Word count:

Sales:
Page Reads:
FREE:

Week of

Goals

Weekly Checklist:

- ☐ Sign up for promos
- ☐ Change prices
- ☐ Order covers
- ☐ Schedule editor
- ☐ Complete edits
- ☐ Upload for sale
- ☐ Send ARCS
- ☐ Set up swaps
- ☐

Monday, 9/24

What to do:

Where to be:

Word count:

Sales:

Page Reads:

FREE:

Tuesday, 9/25

What to do:

Where to be:

Word count:

Sales:

Page Reads:

FREE:

Wednesday, 9/26

What to do:

Where to be:

Word count:

Sales:

Page Reads:

FREE:

September

Thursday, 9/27

What to do:

Where to be:

Word count:

Sales:
Page Reads:
FREE:

Friday, 9/28

What to do:

Where to be:

Word count:

Sales:
Page Reads:
FREE:

Saturday, 9/29

What to do:

Where to be:

Word count:

Sales:
Page Reads:
FREE:

Sunday, 9/30

What to do:

Where to be:

Word count:

Sales:
Page Reads:
FREE:

 # September Notes

What worked?

What changes do you need to make?

What new strategies will you try?

Notes:

October Pep Talk

Yeah, I know. There's still three months of 2018 to finish. One step at a time. Right?

Um. No.

Seriously. Start planning now.

Create a publishing schedule.

How do you know how many books you're going to write?

Well, you can't *for sure,* but you can have a good idea.

It's all about the words, baby.

See, if you have a daily or weekly word count goal, then you know how long it will take you to write a book. You know when to have an editor scheduled. You know when you need that cover. You know when to start marketing. Suddenly, your career is less stressful and you're ahead of the game!

My goal is usually 3k a day. Do I always hit it? No. Because life happens.

Still, I like striving for goals and I'm so much more productive when I know I have an editor waiting on me.

Next year, I'm planning on writing ONE MILLION WORDS.

Uh huh. Sound scary?

What if I told you it was only 2,740 words per day.

Sounds pretty manageable…but what if you only write six days a week because your husband is off and super needy. (Just an example. *cough cough*)

Well, you could have a goal of 19,231 words per week. Completely manageable.

Hey, what if you take two weeks off during the year where you just lived without writing any words. (I don't know how, but I hear people do it.)

That means you only need to write 20k words per week for 50 weeks to accomplish ONE MILLION WORDS.

Oh, and how many books is that? How much would your life change with more books to market and a bigger backlist for readers to devour once they discover you?

Think about it. Then think about 2019.

Hugs.

You've got this!

 # October

Sunday	Monday	Tuesday	Wednesday	Thursday	Friday	Saturday
	1	2	3	4	5	6
7	8	9	10	11	12	13
14	15	16	17	18	19	20
21	22	23	24	25	26	27
28	29	30	31			

Week of

Goals

Weekly Checklist:
- ☐ Sign up for promos
- ☐ Change prices
- ☐ Order covers
- ☐ Schedule editor
- ☐ Complete edits
- ☐ Upload for sale
- ☐ Send ARCS
- ☐ Set up swaps
- ☐

Monday, 10/1
What to do:

Where to be:

Word count:

Sales:

Page Reads:

FREE:

Tuesday, 10/2
What to do:

Where to be:

Word count:

Sales:

Page Reads:

FREE:

Wednesday, 10/3
What to do:

Where to be:

Word count:

Sales:

Page Reads:

FREE:

October

Thursday, 10/4

What to do:

Where to be:

Word count:

Sales:
Page Reads:
FREE:

Friday, 10/5

What to do:

Where to be:

Word count:

Sales:
Page Reads:
FREE:

Saturday, 10/6

What to do:

Where to be:

Word count:

Sales:
Page Reads:
FREE:

Sunday, 10/7

What to do:

Where to be:

Word count:

Sales:
Page Reads:
FREE:

Week of

Goals

Weekly Checklist:
- ☐ Sign up for promos
- ☐ Change prices
- ☐ Order covers
- ☐ Schedule editor
- ☐ Complete edits
- ☐ Upload for sale
- ☐ Send ARCS
- ☐ Set up swaps
- ☐

Monday, 10/8
What to do:

Where to be:

Word count:

Sales:

Page Reads:

FREE:

Tuesday, 10/9
What to do:

Where to be:

Word count:

Sales:

Page Reads:

FREE:

Wednesday, 10/10
What to do:

Where to be:

Word count:

Sales:

Page Reads:

FREE:

October

Thursday, 10/11

What to do:

Where to be:

Word count:

Sales:
Page Reads:
FREE:

Friday, 10/12

What to do:

Where to be:

Word count:

Sales:
Page Reads:
FREE:

Saturday, 10/13

What to do:

Where to be:

Word count:

Sales:
Page Reads:
FREE:

Sunday, 10/14

What to do:

Where to be:

Word count:

Sales:
Page Reads:
FREE:

Week of

Goals

Weekly Checklist:

- [ ] Sign up for promos
- [ ] Change prices
- [ ] Order covers
- [ ] Schedule editor
- [ ] Complete edits
- [ ] Upload for sale
- [ ] Send ARCS
- [ ] Set up swaps
- [ ]

Monday, 10/15

What to do:

Where to be:

Word count:

Sales:

Page Reads:

FREE:

Tuesday, 10/16

What to do:

Where to be:

Word count:

Sales:

Page Reads:

FREE:

Wednesday, 10/17

What to do:

Where to be:

Word count:

Sales:

Page Reads:

FREE:

October

Thursday, 10/18

What to do:

Where to be:

Word count:

Sales:
Page Reads:
FREE:

Friday, 10/19

What to do:

Where to be:

Word count:

Sales:
Page Reads:
FREE:

Saturday, 10/20

What to do:

Where to be:

Word count:

Sales:
Page Reads:
FREE:

Sunday, 10/21

What to do:

Where to be:

Word count:

Sales:
Page Reads:
FREE:

Week of

Goals

Weekly Checklist:
- ☐ Sign up for promos
- ☐ Change prices
- ☐ Order covers
- ☐ Schedule editor
- ☐ Complete edits
- ☐ Upload for sale
- ☐ Send ARCS
- ☐ Set up swaps
- ☐

Monday, 10/22
What to do:

Where to be:

Word count:

Sales:

Page Reads:

FREE:

Tuesday, 10/23
What to do:

Where to be:

Word count:

Sales:

Page Reads:

FREE:

Wednesday, 10/24
What to do:

Where to be:

Word count:

Sales:

Page Reads:

FREE:

October

Thursday, 10/25

What to do:

Where to be:

Word count:

Sales:
Page Reads:
FREE:

Friday, 10/26

What to do:

Where to be:

Word count:

Sales:
Page Reads:
FREE:

Saturday, 10/27

What to do:

Where to be:

Word count:

Sales:
Page Reads:
FREE:

Sunday, 10/28

What to do:

Where to be:

Word count:

Sales:
Page Reads:
FREE:

Week of

Goals

Weekly Checklist:
- ☐ Sign up for promos
- ☐ Change prices
- ☐ Order covers
- ☐ Schedule editor
- ☐ Complete edits
- ☐ Upload for sale
- ☐ Send ARCS
- ☐ Set up swaps
- ☐

Monday, 10/29
What to do:

Where to be:

Word count:

Sales:

Page Reads:

FREE:

Tuesday, 10/30
What to do:

Where to be:

Word count:

Sales:

Page Reads:

FREE:

Wednesday, 10/31
What to do:

Where to be:

Word count:

Sales:

Page Reads:

FREE:

November

Thursday, 11/1

What to do:

Where to be:

Word count:

Sales:
Page Reads:
FREE:

Friday, 11/2

What to do:

Where to be:

Word count:

Sales:
Page Reads:
FREE:

Saturday, 11/3

What to do:

Where to be:

Word count:

Sales:
Page Reads:
FREE:

Sunday, 11/4

What to do:

Where to be:

Word count:

Sales:
Page Reads:
FREE:

 October Notes

What worked?

What changes do you need to make?

What new strategies will you try?

Notes:

The Dangers of Autopilot

For the past month or so, I've seriously been functioning on autopilot in an effort to keep my head above water. Why do I share this? Oh, because in a community full of ambitious, determined, creative women, I know I can't be alone.

Autopilot has its benefits. With the routine, I've been able to accomplish many things I might not have been able to do in the past. For example, I now force myself to take time to exercise five mornings a week while the little one is in school. I have no idea how this will work during the long term or during vacations, but I expect Thanksgiving break will serve to be an awesome test run. By doing this, I've managed to lose over 15lbs in about a month and a half. (I know. Doesn't sound like much, but I'm 45 years old and it would actually be easier for me to move a scale with a bulldozer than to drop pounds at this stage in life. My metabolism actually laughs at me and calls me names. Not nice.)

For the past month or so, I've had my routine of doing the newsletter and making videos, answering questions, struggling to fit in some words. I've been slack. I haven't done the promoting I need to of my own work, mostly because I'm an idiot who joined not one, not two, but SIX boxed sets this year for a variety of reasons...the quest for letters, the desire to work with some wildly talented authors, and my cover designer's charity set. Needless to say, it has been all about writing for those sets and not for my brand.

Autopilot, aka survival mode, has kept me from losing my mind. I'm hanging in there.

The downside: I'm not growing. I'm not pushing past barriers and doing more. Instead, I'm hitting the wall and thrilled to have reached it. Settling into complacency is a terrible idea when there are goals to achieve.

So, now that I'm aware of the problem, I'm going to be shutting off autopilot. Then, I'm going to be pushing. I hope to see you pushing with me.

We've gotta keep growing! There year isn't over yet. There are still goals to achieve and even exceed. Let's get there together. Success is best when shared with friends.

 *November*

Sunday	Monday	Tuesday	Wednesday	Thursday	Friday	Saturday
				1	2	3
4	5	6	7	8	9	10
11	12	13	14	15	16	17
18	19	20	21	22	23	24
25	26	27	28	29	30	31

Week of

Goals

Weekly Checklist:
- ☐ Sign up for promos
- ☐ Change prices
- ☐ Order covers
- ☐ Schedule editor
- ☐ Complete edits
- ☐ Upload for sale
- ☐ Send ARCS
- ☐ Set up swaps
- ☐

Monday, 11/5

What to do:

Where to be:

Word count:

Sales:

Page Reads:

FREE:

Tuesday, 11/6

What to do:

Where to be:

Word count:

Sales:

Page Reads:

FREE:

Wednesday, 11/7

What to do:

Where to be:

Word count:

Sales:

Page Reads:

FREE:

November

Thursday, 11/8

What to do:

Where to be:

Word count:

Sales:

Page Reads:

FREE:

Friday, 11/9

What to do:

Where to be:

Word count:

Sales:

Page Reads:

FREE:

Saturday, 11/10

What to do:

Where to be:

Word count:

Sales:

Page Reads:

FREE:

Sunday, 11/11

What to do:

Where to be:

Word count:

Sales:

Page Reads:

FREE:

Week of

Goals

Weekly Checklist:

- [ ] Sign up for promos
- [ ] Change prices
- [ ] Order covers
- [ ] Schedule editor
- [ ] Complete edits
- [ ] Upload for sale
- [ ] Send ARCS
- [ ] Set up swaps
- [ ]

Monday, 11/12

What to do:

Where to be:

Word count:

Sales:

Page Reads:

FREE:

Tuesday, 11/13

What to do:

Where to be:

Word count:

Sales:

Page Reads:

FREE:

Wednesday, 11/14

What to do:

Where to be:

Word count:

Sales:

Page Reads:

FREE:

November

Thursday, 11/15

What to do:

Where to be:

Word count:

Sales:
Page Reads:
FREE:

Friday, 11/16

What to do:

Where to be:

Word count:

Sales:
Page Reads:
FREE:

Saturday, 11/17

What to do:

Where to be:

Word count:

Sales:
Page Reads:
FREE:

Sunday, 11/18

What to do:

Where to be:

Word count:

Sales:
Page Reads:
FREE:

Week of

Goals

Weekly Checklist:
- [ ] Sign up for promos
- [ ] Change prices
- [ ] Order covers
- [ ] Schedule editor
- [ ] Complete edits
- [ ] Upload for sale
- [ ] Send ARCS
- [ ] Set up swaps
- [ ]

Monday, 11/19
What to do:

Where to be:

Word count:

Sales:

Page Reads:

FREE:

Tuesday, 11/20
What to do:

Where to be:

Word count:

Sales:

Page Reads:

FREE:

Wednesday, 11/21
What to do:

Where to be:

Word count:

Sales:

Page Reads:

FREE:

November

Thursday, 11/22

What to do:

Where to be:

Word count:

Sales:
Page Reads:
FREE:

Friday, 11/23

What to do:

Where to be:

Word count:

Sales:
Page Reads:
FREE:

Saturday, 11/24

What to do:

Where to be:

Word count:

Sales:
Page Reads:
FREE:

Sunday, 11/25

What to do:

Where to be:

Word count:

Sales:
Page Reads:
FREE:

Week of

Goals

Weekly Checklist:

- ☐ Sign up for promos
- ☐ Change prices
- ☐ Order covers
- ☐ Schedule editor
- ☐ Complete edits
- ☐ Upload for sale
- ☐ Send ARCS
- ☐ Set up swaps
- ☐

Monday, 11/26

What to do:

Where to be:

Word count:

Sales:

Page Reads:

FREE:

Tuesday, 11/27

What to do:

Where to be:

Word count:

Sales:

Page Reads:

FREE:

Wednesday, 11/28

What to do:

Where to be:

Word count:

Sales:

Page Reads:

FREE:

November

Thursday, 11/29

What to do:

Where to be:

Word count:

Sales:

Page Reads:

FREE:

Friday, 11/30

What to do:

Where to be:

Word count:

Sales:

Page Reads:

FREE:

Saturday, 12/1

What to do:

Where to be:

Word count:

Sales:

Page Reads:

FREE:

Sunday, 12/2

What to do:

Where to be:

Word count:

Sales:

Page Reads:

FREE:

 # November Notes

What worked?

What changes do you need to make?

What new strategies will you try?

Notes:

Leap.

I love this scene from *Under the Tuscan Sun* where the realtor is telling Diane Lane's character the story of the railroad. They built the track before there was ever a train that could make the journey because they knew there would be one someday.

What do I take from this?

We must prepare for success. When I started Love Kissed Books, LLC on January 1, 2016, I had 200 author emails. Now, I have over three thousand authors who receive my weekly emails about promotions. Not everyone takes advantage of the opportunities here, but they aren't unsubscribing either.

So, how do I explain the growth? I prepared for success. I did everything I could to grow. Every promotion we offer is designed to address the challenges we face as authors. (Yes, I'm an author too. I've been publishing since 2013 and have survived countless twists and turns in the market, which helps me help all of you.)

If you're using this planner, it's because you want to grow. Don't let anything stop you. I mean it. You need to remember your why.

Why are you doing this? Why are you working so hard?

Don't be a lurker in this lifestyle. Take action. Make a list even if you only have two emails on it. Build a Facebook page even if you only know three people who might like it. Create a Twitter even if you don't know what you could possibly say in 140 characters.

Then join some promotions even if you only have one book. (May I recommend those from Love Kissed Books?)

Every month we offer:

1. FREE for All, designed to get downloads/page reads and grow social media

2. Nothing But 99 Giveaway, designed to sell books and grow your Twitter

3. KU Giveaway, designed to bring awareness to your KU books and grow your social media

4. Preorder Promotion, designed to push preorders on Amazon and grow your social media

5. Grow Team Giveaway to grow your review or street team

Periodically we offer:

1. List building opportunities, designed to grow your email list

2. Facebook Hops, designed to grow your FB page and your email list

And these are just the promotions. We also offer a variety of daily newsletters for bargains and freebies, among a host of others.

Have questions? Ask! We're here to help. Nothing would make me happier than to help everyone making a living doing what they love.

December

Sunday	Monday	Tuesday	Wednesday	Thursday	Friday	Saturday
						1
2	3	4	5	6	7	8
9	10	11	12	13	14	15
16	17	18	19	20	21	22
23/30	24/31	25	26	27	28	29

Week of

Goals

Weekly Checklist:

- ☐ Sign up for promos
- ☐ Change prices
- ☐ Order covers
- ☐ Schedule editor
- ☐ Complete edits
- ☐ Upload for sale
- ☐ Send ARCS
- ☐ Set up swaps
- ☐

Monday, 12/3

What to do:

Where to be:

Word count:

Sales:

Page Reads:

FREE:

Tuesday, 12/4

What to do:

Where to be:

Word count:

Sales:

Page Reads:

FREE:

Wednesday, 12/5

What to do:

Where to be:

Word count:

Sales:

Page Reads:

FREE:

December

Thursday, 12/6

What to do:

Where to be:

Word count:

Sales:

Page Reads:

FREE:

Friday, 12/7

What to do:

Where to be:

Word count:

Sales:

Page Reads:

FREE:

Saturday, 12/8

What to do:

Where to be:

Word count:

Sales:

Page Reads:

FREE:

Sunday, 12/9

What to do:

Where to be:

Word count:

Sales:

Page Reads:

FREE:

Week of

Goals

Weekly Checklist:

- ☐ Sign up for promos
- ☐ Change prices
- ☐ Order covers
- ☐ Schedule editor
- ☐ Complete edits
- ☐ Upload for sale
- ☐ Send ARCS
- ☐ Set up swaps
- ☐

Monday, 12/10

What to do:

Where to be:

Word count:

Sales:

Page Reads:

FREE:

Tuesday, 12/11

What to do:

Where to be:

Word count:

Sales:

Page Reads:

FREE:

Wednesday, 12/12

What to do:

Where to be:

Word count:

Sales:

Page Reads:

FREE:

December

Thursday, 12/13

What to do:

Where to be:

Word count:

Sales:
Page Reads:
FREE:

Friday, 12/14

What to do:

Where to be:

Word count:

Sales:
Page Reads:
FREE:

Saturday, 12/15

What to do:

Where to be:

Word count:

Sales:
Page Reads:
FREE:

Sunday, 12/16

What to do:

Where to be:

Word count:

Sales:
Page Reads:
FREE:

Week of

Goals

Weekly Checklist:
- [ ] Sign up for promos
- [ ] Change prices
- [ ] Order covers
- [ ] Schedule editor
- [ ] Complete edits
- [ ] Upload for sale
- [ ] Send ARCS
- [ ] Set up swaps
- [ ]

Monday, 12/17
What to do:

Where to be:

Word count:

Sales:

Page Reads:

FREE:

Tuesday, 12/18
What to do:

Where to be:

Word count:

Sales:

Page Reads:

FREE:

Wednesday, 12/19
What to do:

Where to be:

Word count:

Sales:

Page Reads:

FREE:

December

Thursday, 12/20

What to do:

Where to be:

Word count:

Sales:
Page Reads:
FREE:

Friday, 12/21

What to do:

Where to be:

Word count:

Sales:
Page Reads:
FREE:

Saturday, 12/22

What to do:

Where to be:

Word count:

Sales:
Page Reads:
FREE:

Sunday, 12/23

What to do:

Where to be:

Word count:

Sales:
Page Reads:
FREE:

Week of

Goals

Weekly Checklist:
- [ ] Sign up for promos
- [ ] Change prices
- [ ] Order covers
- [ ] Schedule editor
- [ ] Complete edits
- [ ] Upload for sale
- [ ] Send ARCS
- [ ] Set up swaps
- [ ]

Monday, 12/24

What to do:

Where to be:

Word count:

Sales:

Page Reads:

FREE:

Tuesday, 12/25

What to do:

Where to be:

Word count:

Sales:

Page Reads:

FREE:

Wednesday, 12/26

What to do:

Where to be:

Word count:

Sales:

Page Reads:

FREE:

December

Thursday, 12/27

What to do:

Where to be:

Word count:

Sales:
Page Reads:
FREE:

Friday, 12/28

What to do:

Where to be:

Word count:

Sales:
Page Reads:
FREE:

Saturday, 12/29

What to do:

Where to be:

Word count:

Sales:
Page Reads:
FREE:

Sunday, 12/30

What to do:

Where to be:

Word count:

Sales:
Page Reads:
FREE:

End of 2018

Goals

Weekly Checklist:

- ☐ Sign up for promos
- ☐ Change prices
- ☐ Order covers
- ☐ Schedule editor
- ☐ Complete edits
- ☐ Upload for sale
- ☐ Send ARCS
- ☐ Set up swaps
- ☐

Monday, 12/31

What to do:

Where to be:

Word count:

Sales:

Page Reads:

FREE:

Tuesday, 1/1

What to do:

Where to be:

Word count:

Sales:

Page Reads:

FREE:

Wednesday, 1/2

What to do:

Where to be:

Word count:

Sales:

Page Reads:

FREE:

 December Notes

What worked?

What changes do you need to make?

What new strategies will you try?

Notes:

Goals for 2018

Social Media	Number	Goal	Date Achieved
Newsletter Subscribers			
FB Page Likes			
Twitter Follows			
BookBub Follows			
Review Team			
Street Team			

Marketing/Promotion	Current AVG	Goal	Date Achieved
Sales			
Downloads/FREEBIES			
Page Reads			

Author Career	2017	Goal	Date Achieved
# of Books Published			
# of Words Written			

Personal Goals	Date Achieved

Password Keeper

	Site Name	Username	Password
1			
2			
3			
4			
5			
6			
7			
8			
9			
10			
11			
12			
13			
14			
15			
16			
17			
18			
19			
20			
21			
22			
23			
24			
25			
26			
27			
28			
29			
30			

Publishing

Title	Word Count	Pub Date	Draft Due	Which Editor

Planner

Edit Date	Cover Designer	Design Date	Formatter	Format Date

New Release

Title	KU or Wide	Preorder?	Graphic Teasers/GIF	NL Swaps Scheduled

Planner

Reveal Date	Organizer	Tour Date	Organizer	ARCs?

New Release

Title	Cover Cost	Edit Cost	Graphics Cost	Formatting Cost

Tracker

Reveal Cost	Tour Cost	Ad/Misc Marketing	Total	1st Week Gross	1st Month Gross	Profit/Loss

New Release Pep Talk

You did it! You survived a new release!

This is the scariest part of being an author. We spend countless hours, days, weeks, sometimes even months to create the best possible product. We find the right cover designer to give our book baby the right look. We find the right editor to make sure we use the best word, grammar, and punctuation. Our betas have given it some love. The book was formatted and blurbed. Finally, we hit the button.

There were reviews. There were purchases. There were page reads.

Maybe the results were awesome and we used the tracker to discover we did better than expected. Go you! Maybe the results were less than stellar and we're questioning whether we should even publish again. Stop it. I mean it. Stop right now.

Self-doubt is natural, but pointless. Self-reflection is where it's at. Take a serious look at what you can do differently to have better results next time. Maybe there's a way to cut your expenses. Maybe you have other options for marketing you can try this time. Maybe you need to slow down, not rush things, and grow your social media.

Along the way you, you need to remember: this isn't the last book you're ever going to release. If you are truly passionate about being an author, it's not. You couldn't stop writing for anything. Words are your life. Without them, you're incomplete.

Why do I tell you this?

This is where we pull it all together. Life is a cha cha. You move forward and back. No big deal. Sometimes you win, sometimes you learn. No matter what, don't quit. Don't give up. Simply find ways to improve EVERY TIME.

I've said it before and I'll say it again. This is a marathon, not a sprint. Take your time. Embrace the process. Most of all…pay attention and measure everything. This is how you learn what works, what doesn't, and what you can do better.

Give yourself time to grow. You can do this. Now dust yourself off and go do it again.

New Release Notes

Did you publish profitably?

What changes do you need to make?

What new strategies will you try?

Notes:

Marketing Research

How does your cover compare to covers in Amazon's Top 100 in the same Genre?

Did you write to market? Did you follow the tropes?

How does your blurb compare?

Notes:

Newsletter Swap Info

Ready to master one of the best FREE methods of marketing?

Welcome to Newsletter Swaps 101.

The goal:

1. Find authors in your genre who are either releasing a book around the same time or have a book on sale or priced about the same as yours.

**Please note: in your genre is key!

2. Exchange information.

I like to use Google forms to collect the information. Here's a screenshot of how I set it up:

Newsletter Swap for Contemporary Romance/Erotica

Hello, authors!

I have a boxed set I'm offering for FREE from 3/24-28. I'd love to support those free days with some newsletter swaps.

Looking for books that are also FREE...or 99 Pennies.

Since my FREE days are set, I'd need you to commit to sharing from 3/24-28. I'll share on the date you request.

Some stats:

Author Newsletter Size: 31k +

Let's make this happen.

Questions? Contact Nicole: support@lovekissedbooks.com

I collect the following information:

* Contact Name
* Email
* Author Name
* Title
* Genre (We should match)
* ASIN
* Price
* Date they want me to share (I offer options)
* Date they will share mine (Again…I offer options)

By using Google Forms, you have a way to keep track of all the swaps. You can organize by date you're sharing. You can add columns for notes. If you don't, you can still track on your own, but it's more time consuming and messy. Either way, make sure to add newsletter swaps to your marketing arsenal.

Newsletter Swap Organizer

Title	Author	ASIN	Price	Date Sharing

Swap Tracker

Date Your Book is Shared	Size of List	Proof	Results

About Love Kissed Books, LLC

On January 1, 2016 Love Kissed Book Bargains was born.

The plan was to create a site where authors could advertise their books without spending a fortune, a BookBub-esque site for the common romance author.

We started with newsletter blasts, then expanded to promotions. Currently, we run five to eight promotions each month, designed to help authors sell books, find new readers, and grow their social media.

Our mission from the first day was to help authors. We knew if we focused on making our authors successful and helping them grow, we'd build a business we could be proud of, a place where everyone could grow in the sunshine. With this plan in mind, we've expanded our offerings to now encompass coaching, courses, and printables too! We even have several genre specific sister sites for authors to work with.

If you believe that the author business is better together and success is best when shared, then come learn and grow with us. We'd love to help you achieve your goals.

Love Kissed Directory

| | | | | Preferred | |
| | | | Contact | Method of | |
Site Name	Link		Name	Contact	Email
Link to My Spreadsheet	https://docs.google.com/spreadsheets/d/1AKc6-V0H0O66UukRl3sYIUOXr4Lyf_u-Oa1RoAJycms/edit?usp=sharing				
Love Kissed Book Bargains (LKBB) *for all romance genres $2.99 or less*	http://lovekissedbookbargains.com		Nicole Andrews Moore	FB Message	support@lovekissedbooks.com
Facebook Page	https://www.facebook.com/LoveKissedBookBargains/				
Facebook Author Group	https://www.facebook.com/groups/LoveKissedAuthorPromotions/				
Author Newsletter	http://madmimi.com/signups/180207/join				
Newsletter Blast Sign Up	http://lovekissedbookbargains.com/book-us-now/				
FREEBIES Newsletter Blast	http://lovekissedbookbargains.com/book-us-now/				
Submit New Releases	http://lovekissedbookbargains.com/submit-new-release/				
Love Kissed Coachables	http://lovekissedbookbargains.com/love-kissed-coachables/				
Twitter	https://twitter.com/lovekissedbooks				
Instagram	@lovekissedbookbargains				
Boxed Romance Bargains (BRB) *for collections, anthologies, and boxed sets $2.99 or less*	http://boxedromancebargains.com		*Heather Myers*		
Facebook Page	https://www.facebook.com/boxedromancebargains/				
Newsletter Blast Sign Up	http://boxedromancebargains.com/index.php/author-sign-up/				
Twitter	https://twitter.com/boxed_romance				

PUF Bargains (PUF) *for paranormal, urban fantasy, & Sci-Fi romance $2.99 or less*	http://paranormalurbanfantasybargains.com	*Brandy Dorsch*	Email	paranormalbargains@gmail.com
Facebook Page	https://www.facebook.com/paranormalandurbanfantasybargains/			
Facebook Author Group	https://www.facebook.com/groups/1110703415695214/			
Newsletter Blast Sign Up	http://paranormalandurbanfantasybargains.com/index.php/author-sign-up/			
Twitter	https://twitter.com/pufbargains			
Love Kissed Suspense (LKS) *for romantic suspense and dark romance $2.99 or less*	http://lovekissedsuspense.com	*Brandy Dorsch*	Email	paranormalbargains@gmail.com
Facebook Page	https://www.facebook.com/lovekissedsuspense/			
Facebook Author Group	https://www.facebook.com/groups/lovekissedsuspenseauthors/			
Newsletter Blast Sign Up	http://lovekissedsuspense.com/index.php/author-sign-up/			
Twitter	https://twitter.com/LKSuspense			
Love Kissed Cozies (LKC) *for cozy mysteries $2.99 or less*	http://lovekissedcozies.com	*Tracey Pedersen*	email	lovekissedcosies@gmail.com
Facebook Page	https://www.facebook.com/LoveKissedCozies/			
Facebook Author Group	https://www.facebook.com/groups/LoveKissedCozyAuthors/?fref=nf			
Newsletter Blast Sign Up	http://lovekissedcozies.com/author-sign-up/			
Submit New Release	http://lovekissedcozies.com/author-sign-up/new-releases/			
Twitter	https://twitter.com/LoveKissedCozy			
Sweet Romance Bargains (SRB) *for sweet/clean romancs $2.99 or less*		*Heather Myers*		
Facebook Page				
Facebook Author Group	https://www.facebook.com/groups/1953851768194709/			
Newsletter Blast Sign Up				
Twitter				

Steamy Book Bargains (SBB) *for steamy romance $2.99 or less*	http://steamybookbargains.com	*Monica Corwin*
Facebook Page	https://www.facebook.com/SteamyBookBargains/	
Facebook Author Group	https://www.facebook.com/groups/steamybookbargains/	
Newsletter Blast Sign Up	http://steamybookbargains.com/index.php/2016/12/13/author-sign-up/	
Twitter	https://twitter.com/lovekissedsteam	

Need a list of promotion sites?

Monica Corwin has created a Google Spreadsheet that can help!

Reach out to her: monicacorwin@outlook.com

www.ingramcontent.com/pod-product-compliance
Lightning Source LLC
Chambersburg PA
CBHW082328220526
45470CB00008B/2442